HER INFINITE VARIETY

Poems, Stories, and Plays by

Malcolm Glass

Finishing Line Press
Georgetown, Kentucky

HER INFINITE VARIETY

*Age cannot wither her
nor custom stale
her infinite variety . . .*

    *Enobarbus,
    speaking of Cleopatra*

        Antony and Cleopatra. II, ii

Copyright © 2024 by Malcolm Glass
ISBN 979-8-88838-745-0 First Edition
All rights reserved under International and Pan-American Copyright Conventions.
No part of this book may be reproduced in any manner whatsoever without written permission from the publisher, except in the case of brief quotations embodied in critical articles and reviews.

ACKNOWLEDGMENTS

The author would like to thank these magazines for permission to republish some of the works in this collection:

The Showbear Family Circus: "Her Journey"
Writing in a Woman's Voice: "Stepmom"
Fresh Words: "Staring" (as "The Moves")
The Write Launch: "Elfie's Time Theory," (as "Elfie's Quantum Thoughts"), "Elfie's Christmas Gift"
MacQueen's Quinterly: "Gone"
The Dead Mule School of Southern Literature: "The Last Time He Tried"
Alternating Current: "Shaken and Rooted"
Change 7: "Knowing" (as a prose poem)
Rockvale Review "Crossing"

Publisher: Leah Huete de Maines
Editor: Christen Kincaid
Cover Art: Katharine Tolleson
Author Photo: Malcolm Glass
Cover Design: Elizabeth Maines McCleavy

Order online: www.finishinglinepress.com
also available on amazon.com

Author inquiries and mail orders:
Finishing Line Press
PO Box 1626
Georgetown, Kentucky 40324
USA

Contents

Plot Points

Her Journey 1
Stepmom 3
Goddess of the Garden 5
His Shirt 6
Moving 7

Characters

Rebecca 11
Millicent 12
Staring 13
Elfie's Time Theory 15
Elfie's Christmas Gift 16

Monologues

The High Priestess 19
Siren Song 20
Landing in a New Nest at the LQ Lounge 21
The Last Time He Tried 22
Shaken and Rooted 23

Resolution

Gone 27
Anniversary 28
Knowing 30
Lovers 31
Crossing 32

Plot Points

Her Journey
> — *for Charla*

Two brown eyes, framed by sprays
of pine needles, stared, blinked.
The fawn lowered her head.

This is a once-in-a-life, she thought,
as she lifted the camera to her eye.
The camera strap rustled, and the deer

bolted. Her mama quickly herded her
away. In the viewfinder the focusing
dots nervously flickered trying

to find those eyes. Gone. Lost.
Yet another missed chance.
She lowered the camera and walked

down the gentle slope, listening
to the whispers of high meadow grass
as it brushed past her boots.

In the dry creek bed an ancient
pick-up lay on its back, like a beetle
too weak to right itself, a collage

of rust, paint, and grease, its tires
gone to sun rot. In the finder
she saw a ragged metal carcass

dissolving in slow motion
into a blend of rocks, bark scraps,
bronze leaves, saw-toothed

flakes of steel, a congregation
of twigs and branches. A single
frame could not tell that story.

How many bales had that truck
carried to the feeding troughs?
Half a century ago. She stepped

stone by stone to the other bank
and began the steep climb
up the hill before her, leaving

the truck and its fifty years.
This day fifty years ago: her tenth
birthday. She could still hear

the squeaking of Keds across
linoleum and hardwood, seeking
and hiding. And her first bottle-

spinning kiss, even sweeter now.
Memories like these, she thought,
carry me through the tattered days,

and the days that flow like honey
from a spoon. On the hilltop
crouched a knotty cluster of trees

tangled with vines and brush.
A short walk around the dense
copse with its snag-crazy briars

would bring her to the pasture
and the cows dozing and grazing
in full-fledged sunlight. But easy

pathways had rarely led her
to discoveries she needed.
This was her journey. No one

could tell her the way. Pressing
the camera lens against her red plaid
flannel shirt, she walked straight

into the shadowed heart of the thicket.

STEPMOM

My knock rattled the storm door. My ex-husband's new wife Joann appeared instantly, as though she had been at the window watching my son Trey and me coming up the walk. She was wearing my sweater.

I wanted to say, *That's my sweater, you know*, but, of course, I didn't. I had to be civilized. Besides, it wasn't really my sweater; it was Kevin's, the one I had always worn around the house. I knew why she was wearing it. Kevin keeps the thermostat at sixty-four during the winter.

I said, "Sorry we're late. Rush hour traffic, you know."

"No worry," she said in her nouveau riche lilt. "The lamb roast won't be done 'til six-fifteen." Ah, yes, I thought, You're old school. The way to a man's heart and all that. Kevin will love it. You won't hear whining about under-cooked baked potatoes or over-cooked salmon.

Joann pushed the door open. Trey, dear, how nice to see you."

Trey turned and smiled at me, and we exchanged our secret flutter-blinks. Joann put her arm around Trey's shoulder and pulled him to her.

"I like your shirt, Trey," she said.

He looked up and smiled politely. "Thank you, Joey."

I wanted to tell her, *His father won't. You'll see.* Trey was wearing the gold-and-red- striped polo shirt I gave him on his birthday. Kevin had told me to take it to Good Will, but I didn't. Trey wandered into the house in search of his father, who was hiding from me.

"We'll see you Sunday, then?" She hiked the sweater sleeves up her arms. No need for Kevin to make snide comments about her weight. Or her hair either, thick natural blonde, longer than my mousy mop.

"That's right," I said. "I'll be here at six."

"Good," she said, "We'll take good care of Trey, don't worry."

"I know you will." I closed the storm door and waved goodbye.

As I got in the car, I took a deep breath, glad to be free of her little-girl whine. The car that reached the four-way right after I did, leapt across the intersection, barely missing me. I hit the brakes and the horn, rocked to a stop, and smacked the steering wheel with the palm of my hand.

"Damn idiot!"

I eased on through the intersection as the woman on my right gave me a friendly wave and mouthed sorry. How refreshing. A person with some empathy, a rarity in a world of the self-absorbed and self-satisfied. Like Joann. She seems so happy with herself, secure in her new life, with a sweet boy for a son.

Why was I angry at this woman? What had she ever done to me? She hadn't stolen my husband. He was hers for the taking. And she hadn't broken my home. I had done that myself. I had to get out. I was tired of not being good enough, of failing to be the trophy wife Kevin wanted. After I left, she came along and picked up the pieces.

Jo Ann would be good to Trey, I knew. And that was the heart of my anger, my resentment. She would care for my son and help Kevin, with his fat salary, spoil him. I would end up the weekend mom, the here-again-there-again mom, the real step-mom.

Goddess of the Garden
 —for Mitzi

The morning glories are falling
again, and she's whispering
cuss words to the bamboo pole
slopped over in its muddy trench.

She pulls it back to lift the netting
and the labyrinthine mat and tangle
of vines. The glories nod as though
they understand her frustration.

With the help of cinder blocks
she has the frail wall of leaves
and blooms flying straight again.
She smiles, gives thanks, and offers

praise to the sapling trunk buried
deep enough to hold. So dire,
these tribulations and trials
of my goddess of the garden,

caretaker of stem, leaf, petiole,
and the myriad blooming geometries
of aster, dahlia, marigold, the colors
in gamut, the plumb bob of peppers,

gravid tomatoes. She is, deep down,
like this garden, falling, faltering,
yet unfolding rich and sure,
my Eve, keeper of forgotten Eden.

HIS SHIRT

Charla put her keys on the kitchen table next to the mail Jeremy had brought in. Amber strolled in from the bedroom and rubbed her tail against Charla's calf. She scooped up her tabby, hugged and kissed her. "Did Brenda take good care of my baby?" Amber wiggled to get down. "I know. You're mad at me for leaving you alone. I'm sorry." She shuffled through the mail. So many cards. She had never gotten so much mail, not even at Christmas.

Christmas. Only six weeks away. Then three more weeks to Andy's birthday. He would have been twenty-eight, a number she knew would always haunt her.

She sat down at the table, afraid that a simple act like pushing the toaster back into place on the counter would bring her the smells of warm bread and coffee or the snappy odor of frying onions. She could not let that happen.

Brenda had said, "Let me stay with you for a while, a few nights anyway." But Charla told her she had to do this alone.

Amber swaggered back into the room, and Charla got the bag of food out of the cabinet and scooped a handful of little reddish-brown crosses into the dish. She ran her hand down Amber's back. The cat twitched her tail left-right, turned and came back for more.

Shadows of bare trees carved the scraggly lawn with dark bones. How many times had she stood at the sink peeling carrots or washing potatoes, watching the darkness pull the color from the lawn? Not many times, really. That was going to help. Not many. That was going to make it harder.

Amber wandered into the laundry room to take a nap in a basket of clothes, and Charla followed. "I'm sorry, honey. No clothes to nest in." Her voice sounded hollow in the cold room.

A box of detergent sat on the dryer and, around it, blue granules of soap, scattered across the shining white field. "I'll fix a bed for you, Punkin." She lifted the clothes out of the dryer and put them in a basket. In the tumble of clothes, she found a satin nightgown tangled in Andy's blue-striped shirt. The air crackled when she pulled them apart. She crumpled the shirt, then let it go. The cloth sprang into life, spilling over her hands. Her throat began to tighten. She couldn't hold back. She pressed the shirt to her face.

Moving

She sat on the creaking wicker chair,
feet on an overturned wastebasket,
one hand lifting a glass of iced tea
to her lips, the other hand casually
elegant in her lap. How strange

to see her life boxed and waiting
for the lift lug and cart to the new
house. Everything she thought
she cared for had turned brown
and cubed, merely straight lines

and planes. Books and spatulas,
lipstick and pliers, photographs,
flannel sheets, cans of cat food,
salad bowls, woolen gloves, all
had become as real as geometry.

In the house by the quiet, chill
stream and the row of ragged pines,
she would unpack and carefully
arrange her ephemeral life and see
lines and cubes become illusion again.

Characters

Rebecca

In the hallway upstairs she caught
her foot on the carpet and balanced
a moment on a shaft of light, wishing

for bright bells at her funeral. Her fall
seemed to unfold a frame at a time,
her life passing like dozens of leaves

seeking the earth. Only a few of them
turned to gaze placidly into her eyes;
Pansies in a small vase, third place

at the Women's Club Flower Show,
a canoe paddle drifting out of reach,
an orchid drooping from a pale

blue strapless gown, her son's
basketball trophy, a broken glass
in a plate of red wine, images

she might not have remembered
had she not fallen. And at the foot
of the stairs she rose and walked

quietly into the kitchen. Wrapping
a few ice cubes in a towel, she pressed
the sharp cold against her right knee.

In the living room she lay down
on the couch. And took in slowly
the first breaths of her new life.

Millicent

Lester left town before Millicent understood
what her body was saying. His Pontiac stayed,
where it had been since the car broke down,
parked in the woods not far from Millie's house,

but far from his. Her trips to and from had to be
quick. Seeing her walking the old gravel road
where she lived with her papa and mama would
never surprise anyone. Then Millicent left, to go

visit her aunt in Poughkeepsie. When she came
back, she took a room in Miss Edison's boarding
house on Martin Street. Every day, she walked
to work at Bob's Market, thinking, along the way,

of Lester's straining shoulders and bony chest
hovering over her, the torn buttonholes,
sweaty hair, dank blood, and the sagging
headliner, her sky every Saturday afternoon.

Her memory would not let go of cigarette
butts on the floorboard, the peppermints
for his kisses, the prickle of the wool seat cover,
the unseen spots her tears left on her sleeve

STARING

AT RISE: PAM and DON sit at opposite ends of a
                    bus stop bench.)

DON
Are you going to Frisbee Beach?

(PAM pulls frisbee from beach bag, drops it back in.)

DON (Cont'd)
You probably go a lot. Me too. Every weekend. Funny, I've never seen you there.

(PAM pulls three weirdly colored wigs from bag, drops them back in.)

DON (Cont'd)
Oh, yeah. I've seen that frizzy one.

PAM
Please stop staring at me.

DON
I wasn't staring.

PAM
You were. You haven't taken your eyes off me.

DON
But I was talking to you.

PAM
Stop staring, coming on to me.

DON
Okay, okay. I'm not.

PAM
How would you like it if I stared at you?

DON
Give me a try.

(PAM turns sideways on bench, stares.)

DON
I like it. It's like someone likes what they see.

PAM
I didn't say I didn't like being stared at. I said to stop.

DON
And I did.

PAM
I know. And I loved it. I felt free.

DON
Free?

(PAM slides up against DON, kisses him.)

PAM
Free to come on to you.

(BLACKOUT)

(END OF PLAY)

Elfie's Time Theory

Elfie tells me everyone has
got time backwards. She peels
an orange and the skin

ribbons a spiral, lightly
bouncing in space. Time, she
says, should be reversed.

The fruit flesh squirts juice
in her eye. Squinting, she says
she should have seen that

coming. She dabs lashes and
cheek with her shirt sleeve.
You know what I mean?

I nod, though I don't. She
eyes me, as if she knows
I'm pretending to. It's like

this, she says. Time's pushing
us forward when we should
be pushing it ahead of us.

I nod, Elfie bites into the orange,
I gather the peeling into a coil
like a sprung moebius strip.

Elfie's Christmas Gift

Elfie broke the coffee mug
she gave me for Christmas,
thrown and fired by our friend

Miggles. I don't care about
the mug, I tell her. It was
the thought that mattered.

I assure her, the thought's still
there. In the pieces. Put them
in a small box and tie a ribbon.

We'll keep it forever. Maybe
bury it. The box, mug, pieces.
It will be our time capsule.

She starts to cry and I wonder
if it's the breaking or what I said.
Though I knew it didn't matter.

Monologues

The High Priestess

A crescent moon rises
at my feet, a fragile cradle
for the earth. Close your eyes.

Be still. My right eye, the full
moon, and my left, the mid-day
sun, both shower your eyelids

with my inner gaze. The path
swathed with shadow leads
to dawn and sunset. The path

yellow with damp leaves
of maples leads to sunrise
and dusk. Be still, and open

your eyes reborn, and listen
to the starlight between them.

Siren Song

My rock is yours, she sang,
pulling him from the waves.
Sting me with your sword,

as I wrap you in pennants
of dark hair and cover you
with sly caresses, barely

grazing your shivering skin.
No escape now, even if I tell
how long I will embrace you.

The quavers of my shimmering
voice trill in your ears, and I hold
you in thrall, with kisses three,

my breath in your knotted hair,
the tug of my dark undertow.

Landing in a New Nest at the LQ Lounge

I'm rocking cheek to cheek on my bar
stool, flapping my black wrap skirt,
flouncing the ruffles on my poet's shirt,
blathering to a bed-tanned nincompoop
to my left, when my eye catches a hand
to my right sliding away my dirty drink.
I turn around to see my thin stem drained,
dangling from slender fingers, my olive
poised between her impeccable teeth
like a caught bullet. I start to say, What the . . .
when her onyx eyes catch and hold mine.
No worry, her voice husky, *I'll fill you up again.*
She flags the femme cocktail chef. *Make it
two more doubles, sweetie. And triple olives.*
She gives me a side-ways smolder look,

then locks my eyes again. But I break
the stare to take her in. Fuchsia A-line
sheath with a dusky shadow in the braless
scoop. A purple tattoo on her shoulder:
Good Witch. She spins away for our drinks,
downtown cleavage singing a rondel
to her twist. I look left as nincompoop slips
slowly off her stool and exits to powder
her nose, her spikes a little nervous. Then
I feel a hoop earring knocking my neck
as a tongue flips my earlobe. Ms. Witchy
whispers, *Be my little goose on a crutch,
and I'll cradle you with my wings.* I breathe,
Yeah, Wicked. Wing me to a feathery flutter.

The Last Time He Tried

My cousin Tom tugged at my skirt belt, played
a crooked tune along my neck, his sly
fingers whispering my breath away.
Head on my shoulder, his tongue butterflied

my ear, his huff and hiss steaming my hair. I
shook my head, pulled his hand out of my blouse
and linked my fingers in his. *Not now. My
mama will find us.* I pecked him on the mouth

to say, that's enough. He hissed, *Let's play house*
and walked his fingers the curve of my back.
South. I squirmed away. North. Up my blouse
fumbling my bra. *Not yours*, I barked. *No shack*

for you! He whined as his hand lingered
assward. I smacked him, gave him the finger.

Shaken and Rooted

Rain dumped the sky, come down
slanty, leaving the stale pond
shooted up with pocks, duckweed
raken askew, the fallow field veined
with rivulets. The tin roof had a lot
to say about it, chattering like a drunk
blatherskite. Through the cob-webbed
window I watched my bald hubby,
Beadhead Bob everyone called him
at the mill, and laughed at how he
could sleep through any damn thing,
all scrunched up on the rattly porch
swing, snoring like a frazzled goat.

Been with, I thought, this pop-eyed
fool more than forty-three years
in this creaking lean of a cabin.
Guess that's a luck I never seed
coming, like this wind-harried storm.
Me and Bob. And sunshine. And rain.
Day rolling after day. And nights,
mellow some, and some sharp, and
others a crooked little tune of loving.

Resolution

Gone

Behind the house, a rust-eaten
Pontiac settles into weeds and red
clay. The wheels are locked
in a speed-torn curve by a ghost
hand on the steering wheel.
On the back seat lies a mildewed,
blood-stained blanket that held
the boy on the way to the hospital.

And then the twisted journey
through a maze of sharp words
Why did you leave it in the car?
Loaded. That's where I've always
kept it! Only the dark river sees
the pistol now. Fog hovering
over the river carries wisps
of blue smoke, still pungent
with powder, into the clouds.
Gone is the only word left.
And neither of them even
whispers it. The bitter chill
of summer fills with glances
searching through the grimy
windows for an escape.

On the warped gray boards
of the porch, a tightly packed
suitcase waits. The sprung-hinged
door stands between them,
their eyes clouded by the haze
of the torn screen. She stares
at the muddy gravel driveway.
He scans sunlight flickering
through nodding poplar leaves.

ANNIVERSARY

When Vera found the panties, she quickly stuck them back under Brett's thermal underwear and closed the drawer. In the bathroom, after a few minutes of crying, she decided to forget what she had seen, knowing she couldn't.

She went into the bedroom, pulled them out of the drawer again, and spread the silky, black undies across her knees. She couldn't have gotten into them when she was seventeen. Scarlet puckered lips adorned the front and across the rear in red, *Tina*.

Back in the bathroom she chided herself for wanting to cry again. She took a deep breath and looked at herself in the mirror, brushing a strand of hair away from her eyes. This was far from her first discovery. But this time it was different. This was the one she had been waiting for. She laid her arm on the basin counter to sweep Brett's shaver, soap, cologne, and toothpaste onto the floor, then stopped when she thought of telling Dr. Martin what she had done.

Vera tucked the panties into her bra. They hung down the front of her blouse like a black flag, with the red lips showing. In the kitchen she pulled them out and clutched them in her fist, then put them on the counter beside the toaster while she sipped her cold coffee.

She had given up long ago trying to keep count of Brett's "flings," as he had called one of his encounters on a business trip. "I came home to you, didn't I?" he had said. "I didn't stay in Cincinnati with her. I came home to you. You're the one I love, Vera. She meant nothing to me. It was just a fling."

She once thought of keeping track some way, maybe making notches in one of her wooden spoons, but she had no idea how many notches to make. It would probably be a number higher than she wanted to think about. Picking up her keys, she stuffed the panties in her purse and went out the door to the garage.

At the Dollar Shoppe, she dropped the festive gift bag on the counter.

The clerk said, "Is this it?"

"This is it."

The cow bell on the door made a clang as she walked into the humid air. In the car she closed her eyes and breathed deeply, as the air-conditioner blew gently through her hair. She turned the key and the thrumming of the engine sounded steady, reassuring.

"That was super, dear. You always make such a wonderful salad." Brett wiped a smear of mustard from the corner of his mouth.

"Thank you. I'm glad you liked it. How was the turkey burger?"

"Freezer burn?"

"Maybe so. Sorry."

He stood up. "It was still good."

"What's the rush?" she asked.

"It's my night with the guys, remember?"

"Oh, yes." She pushed back her plate. "Before you go, I have something for you." She reached under the table, pulled out the bag, two feet high and decorated with pink bubbles floating above two champagne glasses.

"It's not our anniversary . . . Is it?"

"It's going to be a new one."

Knowing

Drizzling rain smears the grime
on the windshield of her car,
while she sits in her purple
turtleneck and blue wool skirt,
waiting in the parking lot,
surrounded by empty parking
spaces. She twists the rearview
reading the flaws he won't notice.

Last Saturday he guided her
down a forgotten road in the state
forest. They had nestled under quilts
in the back of her station wagon,
singing together the single-note
suspension of their first stolen time
together, mid-air and breathless
for the resolution, swift eclipse,
the stuttering flare of a new comet.

A blue Honda sedan swings
into the parking space next to her.
The driver waves and smiles.
As he closes the door of his car,
she stares at the muscles in his arm,
as though she was seeing him
for the first time. In this moment
all she wants is her cheek pressed
against the hair on his chest.

This man, settling into her car,
closing his hand around hers,
knows her, body and heart, as he
knows a Brahms sonata, his hands,
his body, far beyond learning
the notes. He kisses her neck,
burying his face in the fur collar
of her coat, and she already knows
the ending, the stretto pulling
the coda from the woven melodies,
her body falling into the final chords.

LOVERS

AT RISE: BEA and ED (60's) sit in chairs, side by side.

BEA
Ed? I've been wanting to tell you something. Ever since Cindy died last month.

ED
What's that?

BEA
She and I were lovers in college.

ED
Cindy? The fiancé I broke up with my junior year was a Lesbian? I never would have guessed. And then I married her Lesbian lover the summer after we all graduated. What do you know?

BEA
Ed, you know I'm not a Lesbian. We were curious, that's all. I knew I wasn't gay. (beat) I hope you aren't upset.

ED
You know me better than that.

BEA
I do. But I've still been nervous. I've been trying to imagine your reaction.

ED
I don't think I have one.

BEA
What do you mean?

ED
What happened happened. Looking back, I think it was supposed to. Because it has become a part of who we are. And if you accept who we are, you accept everything.

(BLACKOUT)

(END OF PLAY)

Crossing

The whisper of her amber perfume
fills her hair with sunset, as we walk
along the creek. A slender log lies
across the roiling water. Side by side

we cross, I, tightrope-walking,
bark crisp under my bare feet, she,
gingerly stepping from dry stone
to flat rock, her arms seeking

balance in the still air, like a small
wounded bird. On the far side
I stand, my hand waiting for hers,
for the steady climb up the bank.

For seventy years **Malcolm Glass** has published poetry, fiction, non-fiction, and plays His work has appeared in many journals, including *Poetry, Nimrod, The Arizona Quarterly, The Sewanee Review,* and *Prairie Schooner.* Heinemann published his guide to writing poetry, *Important Words* (with Bill Brown); and he is the author of a half dozen books published by Scholastic Books. His books of poetry include *Bone Love, In the Shadow of the Gourd, The Dinky Line,* and *Malcolm Glass: Greatest Hits.* His latest collection of poems, *Mirrors, Myths, and Dreams,* was published by Finishing Line Press in 2018.

Also a playwright, many of Glass's plays have been read and produced by theatre companies in the southeast and beyond. His play *Sisters* was given a reading at La Mama Playhouse in New York, and recently, his play *Mistaken Zygotes,* was produced by Northport Plays, New York, in their Annual One Act Play Festival.

Glass's drawings and art photographs have been juried into dozens of galleries and exhibitions from New York to Los Angeles, including The Hilliard Gallery, Northwind Art, Morean Gallery, and Verum Ultimum. His artwork has been honored with many awards, from Honorable Mention to Best of Show. In 2019 his photograph, "Repose," was awarded First Place in the Yeiser Art Center's exhibition "Art Through the Lens."

Glass co-directed the Creative Writing Program at Austin Peay State University, and for many years served as an editor of *The Cumberland Poetry Review* and as co-editor of *Zone 3 Literary Journal.*

He is a Fulbright Scholar, and a recipient of Stetson University's Distinguished Alumni Award. At Austin Peay State University he was awarded the Distinguished Professor Award and the Richard M. Hawkins Award for Creative Achievement.

As a writer, Glass has been guided by a comment W. H. Auden made to him sixty-three years ago: "The best way to become a good poet is to write oneself through the history of poetry in English." His mentors are the poems of Browning, Yeats, Thomas, Frost, Auden, Nemerov, and Wilbur.

www.ingramcontent.com/pod-product-compliance
Lightning Source LLC
Chambersburg PA
CBHW030226170426
43194CB00007BA/879